This Lovely Body

poems by

Mary Elizabeth Parker

Finishing Line Press
Georgetown, Kentucky

This Lovely Body

Copyright © 2017 by Mary Elizabeth Parker
ISBN 978-1-63534-123-2 First Edition
All rights reserved under International and Pan-American Copyright Conventions.
No part of this book may be reproduced in any manner whatsoever without written permission from the publisher, except in the case of brief quotations embodied in critical articles and reviews.

ACKNOWLEDGMENTS

Kalliope: "After carrying her breath"
Tupelo Quarterly Review: "Brood nest on traffic cone"
Reed Magazine, winner of the Edwin Markham Prize: "Jar "
Kalliope: "Prays"
Pinyon Review: "Animal comforts"
Platte Valley Review: "Such a delicate head"
Chagrin River Review: "Near midnight"
Miss Havisham in Winter, chapbook, FutureCycle Press, 2013: "What's left"
Tusculum Review: "Gifts she'd wish to give"
Stone Canoe: "Bear, salted"

Publisher: Leah Maines

Editor: Christen Kincaid

Cover Art: Mary Elizabeth Parker, detail from "Death of the Mother", 3-D collage. Photo: Ann Lamb

Author Photo: Ann Lamb

Cover Design: Elizabeth Maines

Printed in the USA on acid-free paper.
Order online: www.finishinglinepress.com
       also available on amazon.com

               Author inquiries and mail orders:
                      Finishing Line Press
                        P. O. Box 1626
                Georgetown, Kentucky 40324
                          U. S. A.

Table of Contents

After carrying her breath…1
Caduceus…2
Brood nest on traffic cone…3
Hotel…5
Gathers her forces against cells…6
Abgrund:…7
Animal comforts…8
Such a delicate head…9
Prays…10
Gifts she'd wish to give…11
Like ragazzi let loose…12
Keeps herself clean for sex…13
Twilight spreads…15
Craves to be already asleep…16
Carry water…18
Jar…19
Elephant god…21
Near midnight…22
Tiny nightgowns…23
River stones laid on edge…24
What's left…25
Blood sunset…26
Bear, salted…27
Joining the night…28

for T and P and their girls

After carrying her breath

in its paper sack, careful,
heard her doctor say not simply
plugging a hole—
said, to ignite its predictable
evenings, her lung invited in
leather-boy cells,
twisting their boot-heels, itching
to cry havoc and let slip
the dogs of chewed to death—
So, he will give her paper bag back,
deflating, but with some air.

Caduceus

Inventories her lung—
still inhaling, exhaling.
Performs, yet, her offices:
daughters' hair braided,
spilled milk wiped,
bright weeds arranged
in a jelly glass. Gold light,
a pour of unguent,
bastes the kitchen floor.

The workshop clangs
where her husband
braces blond ribs
to staved, ashy boats
to renew them.
May she lash chemo
to the pole of her will
and force its asp to pierce her.

Brood nest on traffic cone

Comes whole and clear into her eye
the sine curve of an upright pigeon

sat like a totem on an orange traffic cone
upright in the bed of a utility truck;

pigeon head, pigeon eye unmoving,
the truck curving (whitely as water

against the curve of a porcelain sink)
through the parking lot

of this grocery where flies
wash their heads like penitents.

The bird does not alter stance
(wings the shining contained riot

color of mother-of-pearl)
as the truck—bird still wedded to cone—

lumbers juddering onto the street and bears
the nesting bird away. Not seen

if the driver's fat tanned arm out the window
is attached to a man who knows

gestation attempts persevere
on a cone behind his head,

a man whose daughter, six maybe,
this morning jumped off the porch

on her way to school and maybe caught the glint
of the pinpoint eye

focused only on brooding; saw
the funny bird sitting a funny nest

in her daddy's power-truck
he drove home illegally after a hard day—

and knew for pretty much certain
the egg couldn't thrive if unbalanced

from the orange cone—
but if she *told* him would the bird be

routed with a broom (Or could it be
maybe he knows his gray jewel

and drives purposefully all day like a Brinks tout—
the possibility of egg given

what she has no word for: grace?)

Hotel

Wakes in pain from the burning
chemo rash pitting her face.
No moon shoulders through
mist sitting squat on the hotel pool
flared orange at sunset:
her girls pink carp fluttering,
delirious with pleasure.
Chlorine cuts the rush of gardenia
from the black hedges bordering.
Wavering shadows of elms
arc stories above the roof.
She would fold her girls back
into her body
if it were not
such an unsafe house.

Gathers her forces against cells

exploding like pick-up sticks,
tries to hold that scatter
as she leans into the bulwark
of her bones, surveys
what still is standing:
her daughters, coalesced
of the best in her, *milagros*.

Yellow squash blossoms
climb the trellises.
Heat, she hopes,
momentarily throttles
marauders through
her spleen, her lungs.

She'll stop watering
the ornamentals,
to force deep roots.
Garden tendrils into
the yard, yard expands to
the road, road splays to
the horizon where
the hours steam white, stupefied.

Abgrund:
>*from the German: the soil*
>*that is underfoot, from which*
>*it is possible to "strike root and stand"*

Translucent tiny shoot
climbs from the crisper:
three ebullient fisted leaves
small as earwigs, from a limp
carrot in the corner.
In the Dust Bowl, a pigtailed
girl lowered into the well
scooped the last muck-inch of water—
meets on the well-tiles a sluggish snake.
Emanation of thirst all that snake is:
can't yet let herself fail.

Animal Comforts

Digs the wire brush
into the pug's under-coat;
gleans with a metal comb
for clots of hair—
as if she knit miracle
from every ungainly material.
Dried-out hollyhocks sway:
that sick fox (something like a fox)
that yesterday crept to take water
from the dog pan,
skinny-ribbed, paw held lame,
tail a sock-monkey's—
stares it eye-to-eye
(its eyes walled, lithium blue),
stares mute, both
still trying to make a stand.

Such a delicate head

—that child on her tricycle—
lavender scalp
glimpsed through the fine
silvery-blonde hair
whorled in two tight plaits on the skull,
like raised pale veins—coil at the neck,
coil near the right ear.
The girl's expectant mother
curves behind her, hand stopped
before it disturbs a filament of white.
Her hand would reach to touch,
to know the ice beneath such white,
Russian steppes flaring snow.
The girl pedals fast; no language
to call her back. A new one will be born
from the mother's rounded womb.
Outside, the first rhododendrons fold in
with fall, tissued purple as newborn
skin. *Her* hands gather fistfuls
of any stick that grows.

Prays

—when she remembers—
to her female saint:
Tortures of the body not
what I think of
when I think of you;
but peace
dithering down
to the depths of a sun-warmed well,
like a feather loosed
in the yard.
Your hands caught that hen,
wrung and plucked,
rhythm of taking what's
needed and no more.
Blue jacaranda
seeds into the breeze
looping south to Rhodes,
where Knights Templar
await the call
to spring blood in the streets.
You stay home, your gaze
a saucer of oil;
your hands perform
their thousand sleeping acts.
I know of you, vividly, nothing:
breasts on a plate like
little war helmets; but your
day-to-day? Slight
as a finger bone sucked clean.

Gifts she'd wish to give

Concrete poured not quite stiff enough in summer
crumbles with cold to a new confectionery—
divinity airy with holes—sky a milk eye gone bad,
the changes un-remarked as the concrete
which hollows like fat cells emptying
beneath skin. *I love you*, he says, though that
won't be enough; yet the body continues despite
blood flowing pinkish now, non-substantive,
never again so full to bursting that if a whole
ox were discovered, dressed out, they'd laugh and eat,
as if they expected it. What to do? Erect a glass house
with a view of the river—build flush to the flood line,
daring the water to climb and kiss.

Like ragazzi let loose

to skid down polished halls,
cells race through her lungs.

She would like to express milk
through her still-full breasts—

nurse it to the mouth
of that five-year-old

on television: Novemthree,
Malaysian, skull bulged huge

with cytoma.
Yet despite the most loving

embroidery of lasers,
he dies.

She presses violets against
the dam of her mouth.

Keeps herself clean for sex

as he grows
afraid even to brush
her brittle sacrum.
Mermaid scales
glinting from the carpet
from a green sequined
dress she never wore—
Thinks of a friend who
spoiled herself
with bad husbands,
and chafes now, caught
raising two children
for her dead daughter.
Her own sins, venial,
scattered, wink
at her like sequins
from the carpet nap.

Lacy blouse, still
two breasts beneath.
What hurts:
the useless repeating
the history of this,
body open to any doctor,
as if fingertips, glancing,
could heal loss upon loss
collecting like rain
until the blue receptacle of ease
that was her body
empties to a loose embrace
of bone, skin.

Appetite
slaked now on
hummingbird dew,
joke nurturance—
un-cradled egg plucked
negligently as feathers—
given over
to hands doing this
as if to turn in their gyre
were easy.

Twilight spreads

like Gentian violet on a wound.
He appears near her pillow,
offering an apple. Plans,
even the worst nights,
that she will come free of this:
a phosphorescent cave-fish
surfaced, a she-bear
rolled from its cave in Spring,
their daughters squeaking after, and he
blinking in glare
like a beast un-confounded.

Craves to be already asleep

when light drops from the sky,
for dark to just
graze her eyelids, not mould—
a rubber sheet against her face.

Flashed hard fists as a kid
when forced by the girls who
held her baby sister down for boys
(but she couldn't stop that)

and now the weight knees her
own lungs, flattened.
Doesn't wake him, but rises
to the door of her daughters'

small room, reluctant to step
damage inside.
Traces with a fingernail, as if
tracing their sleeping eyelashes,

their Boogie-Bee toy
abandoned on the doorsill:
posed on a tiny red platform,
two upright roly-poly

girl bees, to press
from beneath with a thumb
so the string-jointed bodies
bee-bop, dip and bow.

*We can't expect
happiness all the time*, a curt friend
told her, *and it's silly, believing
this vale is followed by heaven.*

Knows of another good woman
who died much faster than this.
She presses deeply, once.
The bees sag in a low prayer.

Carry water

Shove the nozzle in the gas tank and fill.
But lately, she can't do
necessary things: immobile
last night in the sheets, bound neck to toe
(like a cigarette, rolled)
after her restive foot kicked a body-size hole
where just a tiny rent had been.

Jar

The sauce jar drops—
a proliferating tear
in its molecular chain when it
strikes the kitchen's
unyielding composite
island. Lets loose
a *clink*—clean center break—
and sauce pours red on the floor,
bright food for their four bodies
wasted—but she tries with a spoon
to scrape red pooled
into a near-empty red sauce
from the freezer she is
always trying to anoint
with enough food colors
so she won't dream
(yet wakes, even, to dream it)
the landscape pocked
with small pools of gray ice
where it is unknown which may be
deep enough to drown her.
Some sauce salvaged. But
(washing out the broken
jar halves for the trash, soaping so
spice atoms won't attract dogs
to the Dumpster (yet wraiths of sauce
still spread their wings for a dog's
olfactory, the pug lapping
frenzied at the cleaned floor))
she sees that what she thought was
a whole pieced-together jar
is not yet whole: yields

a thumb-shape half-moon of air
up near the lid. *How?* She scours
island, floor, *then jerks the now-filled
jar from the freezer and
with a colander and careful
fingers strains*
the sauce to quarry:
microscopic glint after glint
with their teeth up, tiny antics
of the demons she knows
control things:

*She would have served this, would have
made them eat glass.* No waking
from a dream of ice in the esophagus:
bleeding in this house where she is
too ill to lean away from inserting
the coy sliver.
She throws the jar away, saves
them, herself, for now.

Elephant god

Rousing herself
from a nodding nap
at the table she tried to clear,
she laughs at the skirl of bagpipes
escorting her from dream.
Late sun burnishes
the varnished cupboard gold,
in the pattern of cupping-glasses
on a feverish back;
blurs molten, pools
as the head of *Ganesha*,
laughing elephant god.

Inside her, some cells still work—
so why not yet deliver
infinite possibility: congeal into
platypus, killdeer, even shining
June-bug, just not this?
She dreamt a lion leapt
the wall, clamped the head
of a paralyzed mother.
She, watching, stepped forward, advised:
Lion's fine. Let it be.

Near midnight

this diner she fled to
(he drives her, though her
lungs shouldn't breathe
public air now) sags
with the breath of the
homeless, near-homeless.
Low prayers
from the girl in the mint-green slip
to the cracked plastic doll
she clutches;
to the boy with a waxed-paper comb
in line who screeches
the keening of whales—
until he's booted out.
Chitin paring of moon
above the plate-glass
re-lights the eyes of Gregory Peck,
slumped, unhitched,
Marooned when his
space umbilical snapped.
Disturbance of chaos
causes chaos:
Drosophila melanogaster,
wrinkle-winged, buzzes dry and
Darwin's daughter Annie dies.

Tiny nightgowns

at the streetlamp are not moths:
Dream boys, white paper bells,
swing down the wet street,
wide as the cloud
skimmed from ear to ear
inside her skull.
Keep yourself in flesh, they say,
while we flit, forgetting.

River stones laid on edge

in the churchyard wall
like saw-teeth

to pin minds to the pure white,
should not be counted over and over.

White roar of gravity working the river,
high rocks to low, shouldn't draw her.

Ash from the maintenance fire pit
may be swept clear so her feet stay clean;

but the mouth and the throat
choke for years.

Some countries sew
dead mouths against leaks,

but slow desiccation's
worse: a little rain

pooled beneath leaf rot,
memory still wet.

At dusk, swifts un-choreographed
mass and wheel above the roof,

dark against dark, up-flung.

What's left

Her white patent boot
flung out in the garden,
singing now in the bracken—
vibration ascribed
to simple things: tilled
earth slipping glacially
chip by mica chip
to white powder, white
song sung through rock—
But not terrible: quiet
thimble leak through dikes
that skim the massing sea.
Still, frantic for
mother-touch, a female
god's voluptuous
midriff, pillow-y vault
to hide the tiny seed
until it can be trotted off
in the magic carriage, saved.

Blood sunset

Barbed-wire fence
flames west, tracks of a surgical scar.
Horse against the wire
curves to its last dressage,
forelegs crumpling.
If she could:
Heap horse over her,
drag it to life—
night's axis a centrifuge
flinging off
death, her fists pounding grief.

Bear, salted

A black bear laboriously, tearfully
hauled from the highway
and skinned prayerfully, slumps
across the kneeling lap of a woman
on TV. The bear's wet-muscled head
tips forward to a second young woman
who leans into it with a field knife.
They want to re-carve
the bear's tenderness:
canines sheathed, up in the gums;
pelt's wide discarded heat
pressed up against
the cold in the room;
neat brown liver on a white plate,
left unassimilated by men
who killed to eat but didn't.
The body moans up from its organs
toward the galaxy's spill of salt.
She thinks, *Do we look like this*
dressed out of our skins:
same pubis and coccyx,
same meaty, short legs bowed in?
Bears are not us,
not worrying these questions—
(just enough us to release a low paean
unto the air we won't matter in again).

Joining the night
    for P
    d. March 18, 2008

not meaning to be other than it is—
but the house pug harooing
can't say what it yips at;
and feral dogs don't know
they chase it;
and ghost-thin foxes
streak through the ditches not knowing.
Night doesn't mean to be
loud as roaches
skittering the lampshades—
deafening as mold's
repeating pinwheels—
more remarked
than the ring-tailed raccoon,
faint damp mound
at the woods opening
she enters now
to another country.

MARY ELIZABETH PARKER's poetry collections include THE SEX GIRL, Urthona Press, and 4 chapbooks: MISS HAVISHAM IN WINTER, FutureCycle Press; CAVE-GIRL, Finishing Line Press; BREATHING IN A FOREIGN COUNTRY, Paradise Press; and THAT STUMBLING RITUAL, Coraddi Publications, University of North Carolina, Greensboro.

Her poems have appeared in NOTRE DAME REVIEW, GETTYSBURG REVIEW, NEW LETTERS, ARTS & LETTERS, CONFRONTATION, MARGIE, PASSAGES NORTH, and GREENSBORO REVIEW (nominated for a Pushcart Prize).

She has been featured poet on POETRY DAILY and in MARGIN: EXPLORING MODERN MAGICAL REALISM, and has twice been a fellow at Vermont Studio Center.

She also writes prose: Her essay "Combat Boots" was nominated for a Pushcart Prize. Her short story "Papier-Mache" was published as part of Papier-Mache Press's anthology *Grow Old Along with Me; The Best Is Yet to Be*, whose audio version was one of only 5 books-on-tape nominated for a national Grammy Award that year (Hillary Clinton's book-on-tape *It Takes A Village* won).

She is creator and chair of the Dana Awards in the Novel, Short Fiction, and Poetry.

www.ingramcontent.com/pod-product-compliance
Lightning Source LLC
LaVergne TN
LVHW041514070426
835507LV00012B/1559